For the *Love* of the Tigers

An A-to-Z Primer for Tigers Fans of All Ages

Foreword by Sparky Anderson

Written by Frederick C. Klein

Illustrated and designed by Mark W. Anderson

The game of baseball has been very good to me, and one of the things I feel the most thankful for is all of the wonderful people I met during my years with the Tigers. You really have to live and work in Detroit to realize that the people there are some of the most generous people in the world. I will always appreciate that as much as the World Series championship we won there back in 1984.

I have always believed it was important for people to give back to the game whenever possible, and a great way to do that is to reach out to younger fans and teach them about the history of baseball. In *For the Love of the Tigers*, Frederick C. Klein and Mark Anderson do a great job of reliving the history of the Tigers in a fun and colorful way.

I think every baseball fan wants to pass down their love of the game to their children, and this book is a great way to do that. Flipping through these pages will remind you of some of your favorite Tigers players and will also teach you and your kids some things you probably didn't know. I hope you enjoy it as much as I did.

–**Sparky Anderson**

"A" is for Anderson,

Who gave his teams spark.
In his years in the dugout
He left a huge mark.

White-haired **George "Sparky" Anderson** ran the Tigers from 1979 through 1995, the longest tenure of any Detroit manager. His 1,331 wins with the club also is a record. A hustling but weak-hitting infielder as a player, he hit his stride in the dugout, guiding Cincinnati's "Big Red Machine" to World Series titles in 1975 and 1976 and repeating the feat with the 1984 Tigers. That Detroit club won 104 regular-season games and steamrolled through its eight playoff contests with seven wins.

"B" is for "The Bird,"

Mark Fidrych by name.
For one memorable season
He lit up the game.

Mark Fidrych was a right-handed pitcher whose gangly build and mass of blond curls earned him the nickname "The Bird" after the Sesame Street character "Big Bird." Fidrych came up with the Tigers in 1976 at age 21 and promptly captivated the majors with dazzling stuff and such antics as talking to the ball and getting down on his hands and knees to smooth the mound. His 19–9 won-lost record and 2.34 earned run average that year earned him an All-Star Game berth and Rookie of the Year honors. Alas, the next season he suffered a shoulder injury, and while he pitched a few more years he never matched his rookie brilliance.

"C" is for Cobb,

Who slid with spikes high.
Between the white lines
He'd never say die.

Ty Cobb was baseball's all-time-best hitter, averaging .367 over 24 major-league seasons (1905–1928), all but the last two with the Tigers. He won 12 American League batting titles and hit .400 or better three times. His career records for hits (4,191) and stolen bases (897) endured for decades after he'd retired. Cobb was a rough and uncompromising competitor who had few friends in the game, even among his own teammates, but set standards for intense play that still are remembered.

"D" is for

Dauss,

Whose nickname was "Hooks."
His victory total
Lives on in the books.

George Dauss was a curveball specialist whose 223 victories (against 182 losses) from 1912 through 1926 remains a Tigers team record. The right-hander had his best year in 1915, when he won 24 games for a team that trailed the Boston Red Sox by just 2½ games in the American League race. That would be the Tigers' best finish until their pennant-winning 1934 season. After he retired from baseball, Dauss became a detective with the Pinkerton Agency.

"E" is for

Evers-

This guy gave a hoot.
He helped put the Tigers
Upon the right route.

Walter "Hoot" Evers, who got his nickname because of his boyhood fondness for the movie cowboy "Hoot" Gibson, signed with the Tigers out of the University of Illinois in 1941. He played one game with the team that season, then marched off to World War II for four years. He returned in 1946 to have a 12-season major-league career, six in Detroit. His best year as a Tiger was 1950, when he hit .323 with 103 RBIs and was an All-Star Game outfield starter for a club that finished second, just three games behind the Yankees. That was as close as the Tigers would come to a pennant until 1967.

"F" is for Freehan,

A rock in a mask.
This U of M guy
Did all you could ask.

Bill Freehan played both baseball and football for the University of Michigan before signing with the Tigers in 1961. He was promoted to the big leagues in 1963 and spent his entire 14-season career in Detroit, making a mark as one of the game's most durable catchers. Freehan was named to 11 All-Star teams and won five Gold Glove Awards. When he retired after 1976, his 1,581 games behind the plate ranked ninth on the all-time list. He later returned to coach baseball at his Ann Arbor alma mater.

"G" is for Greenberg and Gehringer,

Two fellows with pop.
In the '30s they led
The team to the top.

"Hammerin' Hank" Greenberg's booming hits helped the Tigers win pennants in 1934, 1935, 1940, and—after four years of World War II service—1945. The big first baseman posted some eye-popping numbers, including 58 home runs in 1938 and 183 runs batted in—the third-highest one-season total ever—in 1937. **Quiet Charlie Gehringer** was Greenberg's teammate for most of that period. He was the best-fielding second baseman of his era, batted .300 or more in 13 of his 16 full major-league seasons, and collected 2,839 career hits. Greenberg's uniform number 5, and Gehringer's number 2, both were retired in a Tiger Stadium ceremony on June 12, 1983.

"H" is for Harwell_

The fans loved him so,
That when the team sacked him
They rose and cried "No!"

Georgia native **Ernie Harwell** brought his relaxed broadcasting style to Detroit in 1960 and kept it there through 1991, when Tiger management didn't renew his contract. So loud was the popular outcry over his release that in 1993 he was brought back for a decade-long encore by the team's new owner, Mike Ilitch. Among Harwell's signature calls were "Long gone!" for a Tiger home run and "Two for the price of one!" for a double play.

"I" is for Innings,

The standard is nine.
But if the game's tied
Then more are just fine.

"J" is for Jennings,

An old Oriole.
He did what it took
To help teams reach their goal.

Hughie Jennings earned his baseball stripes as a shortstop with the 1890s Baltimore Orioles, a team whose name remains synonymous with gritty play. He stood out among even that hard-nosed bunch by reaching base as a hit-batsman 51 times in 1896, a figure that's never been topped. Jennings managed the Tigers for 14 seasons (1907–1920), leading them to American League pennants in 1907, 1908, and 1909. He was noted for his shouting, whistling, arm-waving sideline antics, designed to distract the opposition. One year he was suspended for blowing a tin whistle while foes batted.

"K" is for Kaline,

Also Kell and Kuehn,
Three of the best players
Detroit's ever seen.

At age 20, in just his second full season in the majors, **Al Kaline** won the 1955 American League batting title with a .340 mark. The right-fielder went on to play in Detroit for 22 years, collect 3,007 hits, and become the most-popular Tiger of his era. **George Kell** manned third base for the team from 1946 through 1952, winning the AL batting crown in 1949 and establishing Hall of Fame credentials. **Harvey Kuehn** was the league's Rookie of the Year as a Tigers shortstop in 1953. He won the batting championship in 1959 and made the All-Star team in each of his eight full seasons with the club.

"L" is for Lolich-

Okay, he was round–
But in the '68 series
He starred on the mound.

Left-hander **Mickey Lolich** was a solid starting pitcher for the Tigers from 1963 through 1975, posting 207 of his 217 career victories with the team. But he never performed better than in the 1968 World Series against the St. Louis Cardinals, in which he started, finished, and won three games, allowing just five runs in all. His 4–1 decision over the Cards' Bob Gibson in the seventh game was a Series classic. Lolich had a rotund figure and joked about it. Said he, "All the fat guys watch me and say to their wives, 'See, there's a fat guy doing okay. Bring me another beer.' "

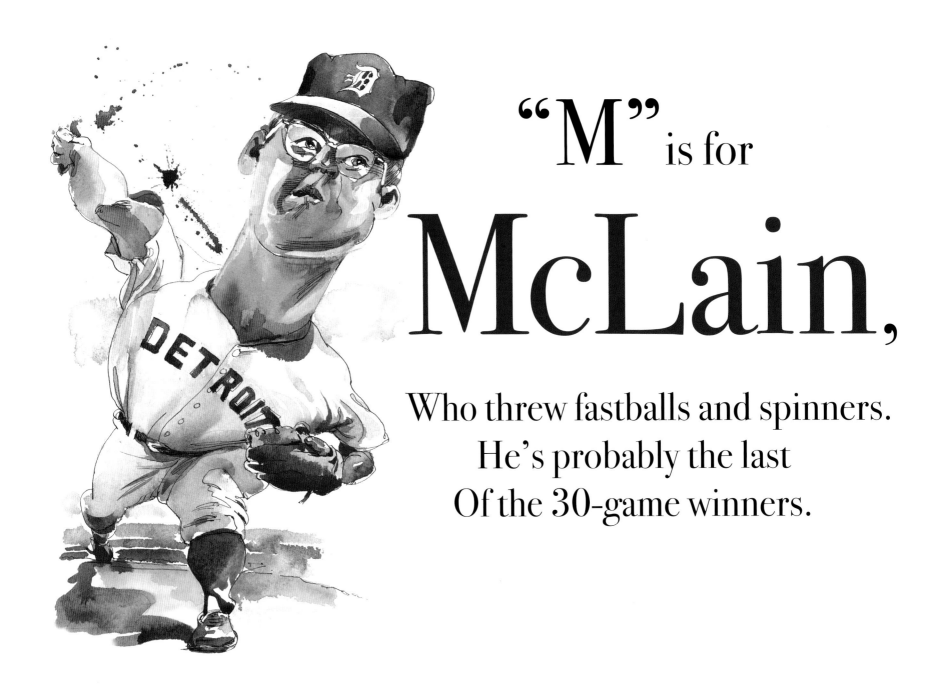

"M" is for McLain,

Who threw fastballs and spinners. He's probably the last Of the 30-game winners.

What Mickey Lolich was to the 1968 World Series, **Denny McLain** was to the Tigers' regular season that year. The sturdy right-hander started 41 games, finished 28 of them, and rang up a 31–6 won-lost record. That was the first 30-or-more-wins season by a pitcher in 34 years. It's also likely to be the last, because today's five-man starting rotations and specialized bullpens don't give pitchers the opportunity to win that many games. McLain had one more good season before being felled by injuries. His post-baseball life has been marred by legal woes, capped by six-year prison term for looting the pension fund of a company he ran.

"N" is for Newhouser,

Who during the war
Kept up the spirits
Of the Motown home corps.

Baseball's quality declined when many players served in the military during the 1941–1945 World War II years, but Detroit native **Hal Newhouser**, who was excused from service because of a heart problem, excelled on the mound during the period and helped bring home a 1945 World Series title. The tall, left-handed "Prince Hal" fought early career wildness before blossoming in 1944 with a 29–9 won-lost record. The next year he went 25–9 and won two games in the World Series against the Chicago Cubs. He put to rest claims he was a "war-years wonder" by posting 26 victories in 1946 and 21 in 1948. He's in the Hall of Fame.

"O" is for Ordonez,

His muscles do ripple.
Was that hit a home run?
Nah, only a triple.

Magglio Ordonez was a proven batsman with power to all fields, but a knee injury that cost him most of the 2004 season made his signing by the Tigers to a long-term contract the next year risky for the team. The risk seemed to increase when he went on the disabled list with another injury early in his first season in Detroit. However, the move paid off in 2006, when "Mags" led the team's pennant drive with 104 runs batted in, and even more then next season when his .363 batting average led the league. He continued his fine play in 2008 by batting .317 with 21 homers and 103 RBIs.

"P" is for Parrish,

Aka "The Big Wheel."
For almost two decades
He was the real deal.

Lance Parrish succeeded Bill Freehan as the Tigers' regular catcher in 1978. He spent the next nine seasons in the post, then went on to play through 1995 with several other major-league teams. Parrish had his best years in Detroit, hitting 212 of his 324 career home runs there, making six All-Star teams, and winning Gold Glove and Silver Slugger awards. The strength of his throwing arm was revealed in the 1982 All-Star Game, when he gunned down three National League runners on the base paths.

"Q" is for Quellich,

Who had just a short look.
But his name starts with "Q"
So he's here in the book.

George Quellich, from Johnsville, California, played with the Tigers for part of the 1931 season. In his only major-league trial the outfielder appeared in 13 games, had 54 official at-bats, and hit .222. This book mostly is about the men who starred for the Tigers, but Quellich's career was typical of many of the almost 1,500 players who have worn the Detroit uniform since 1901. Having played major-league baseball, no matter how briefly, remains a life-long distinction.

"R" is for Rowe,

Who took batters to school.
When he manned the mound
Victory was the rule.

Lynwood "Schoolboy" Rowe, so nicknamed because at age 15 he played with an adult men's team in his native Waco, Texas, was a pitching star for the pennant-winning Tigers clubs of 1934, 1935, and 1940, posting a total of 59 victories in those seasons. Tall, handsome, and folksy, the right-hander was a fan favorite as well. His remark "How'm I doin', Edna?" aimed at his sweetheart and later wife during a national radio interview, became a catchphrase of the era.

"S" is for

Stanley,

Who to get a big win,
Changed his position
From outfielder to "in."

Mickey Stanley was a fixture in center field during most of his 1964–1978 career in Detroit, but as the 1968 World Series approached Tigers manager Mayo Smith didn't think his team could compete with the National League champion St. Louis Cardinals with the weak-hitting Ray Oyler at shortstop—so he moved Stanley there. Stanley never had played short but started all seven Series games at the position in his team's winning effort. He began the next season as a shortstop, but the experiment ultimately failed, and he returned to the outfield.

"T" is for Trammell,

Who with Whitaker, Lou,
Turned many a ground ball,
Into outs one and two.

Shortstop **Alan Trammell** and second-baseman **Lou Whitaker** first played together with the Tigers' minor-league team in Montgomery, Alabama. They teamed up again in the majors in 1978 and for the next 18 seasons formed baseball's best and longest-running double-play combination. Solid hitters as well, they played in 11 All-Star Games between them. Trammell managed the Tigers from 2003 through 2005. Whitaker has been a spring-training instructor for the team.

"U" is for Uhle,

A pitcher with clout.
He'd set the side down
then go hit one out.

Most pitchers are poor hitters but **George Uhle** was an exception. Over 17 big-league seasons (1919–1936), five of them with the Tigers (1929–1933), the right-hander batted .289, the highest lifetime average for someone who only pitched. A 200-game career winner on the mound, his best all-around year was 1923, when he won 26 games and hit .361 for the Cleveland Indians. He is credited with naming the "slider," the half-fastball, half-curve that's a part of most current pitchers' repertoire.

"V" is for Verlander,

This kid came up strong.
And showed Tigers fans
he really belonged.

Few pitchers have had splashier initial major-league seasons than **Justin Verlander.** In 2006, at age 23, the tall right-hander posted a 17–9 won-lost record, started in the World Series, and was voted American League Rookie of the Year. The next season he went 18–6 and threw a no-hitter. He got off to a bad start in 2008 and his won-lost record dipped to 11–17, but he still led the Tiger staff in starts (33), innings pitched (201), and strikeouts (163).

"W" is for Willie—

Mr. Horton, last-named.
For hitting with power
He was justly famed.

Willie Horton, a graduate of Detroit's Northwestern High School, played for 14 seasons with the Tigers (1963–76) and hit the big majority of his 325 career home runs with the team. The outfielder and designated hitter had his best power year in 1968, when his 37 homers helped propel the World Series champions. He's still with the team as special assistant to President David Dombrowski.

"**X**" marks the spot
For a ballpark that's grand.
Comerica Field
Is the best in the land.

Detroiters hated to lose Tiger Stadium, their team's home for 78 years, but they have taken to Comerica Park, which opened with the 2000 season. They proved this in 2007 by topping the 3-million mark in attendance for the first time. The new facility, on Woodward Avenue, seats 41,000 people, has some 70,000 square feet of concession space, and offers striking skyline views beyond center field. Stainless steel statues of Ty Cobb, Charlie Gehringer, Hank Greenberg, Willie Horton, Al Kaline, and Hal Newhouser—by the noted sculptor Omri Amrany—line the left-field concourse, reminding fans of past Tigers glories.

"Y" is for

York,

Not much with a glove,
But with bat in hand was
Someone to love.

Heavyset **Rudy York** was slow afoot and struggled to find a "safe" position in the field during his 12-season career (1937–1948), but he was one of the leading power hitters of his day. His best year was 1940, when his 34 home runs and 134 runs batted in helped the Tigers win the American League pennant. He had 18 homers and 87 RBIs in the championship 1945 season.

"Z"

Is the sound someone makes when he snoozes.
A Tigers fan stays loyal even when his team loses.

World

Tigers in the World Series

1907
Lost to the Chicago Cubs in four games

1908
Lost to the Cubs in five games

1909
Lost to the Pittsburgh Pirates in seven games

1934
Lost to the St. Louis Cardinals in seven games

1935
Beat the Cubs in six games

Series

1940

Lost to the Cincinnati Reds in seven games

1945

Beat the Cubs in seven games

1968

Beat the Cardinals in seven games

1984

Beat the San Diego Padres in five games

2006

Lost to the Cardinals in four games

Purchase high quality 18x24 archival prints and
T-shirts of your favorite Tigers at:

Tigers
baseball
art.com

Triumph Books and colophon are registered trademarks of Random House, Inc.

This book is available in quantity at special discounts for your group or organization. For further information, contact:

Triumph Books
542 South Dearborn Street
Suite 750
Chicago, Illinois 60605
312. 939. 3330
Fax 312. 663. 3557

Printed in China
ISBN 978–1–60078–212–1